WHAT DO
YOU ALLOW TO
DEFINE YOU?

OVERCOMER

BIBLE STUDY

CREATED BY
STEPHEN KENDRICK AND ALEX KENDRICK
BIBLE STUDY DEVELOPED WITH
NIC ALLEN

LifeWay Press® • Nashville, Tennessee

EDITORIAL TEAM

Nic Allen
Writer

Reid Patton
Content Editor

David Haney
Production Editor

Jon Rodda
Art Director

Joel Polk
Editorial Team Leader

Brian Daniel
Manager, Short-Term Discipleship

Michael Kelley
Director, Discipleship and Groups Ministry

Published by LifeWay Press® • © 2019 Kendrick Bros., LLC.
Used under License. All Rights Reserved.

Movie images and photography (pp. 1, 5, 6, 12, 22, 32, 42, 52, 60, 62, 64): AFFIRM Films A Sony Company © 2019 Columbia TriStar Marketing Group, Inc. All Rights Reserved.

No part of this book may be reproduced or transmitted in any form or by any means, electronic or mechanical, including photocopying and recording, or by any information storage or retrieval system, except as may be expressly permitted in writing by the publisher. Requests for permission should be addressed in writing to Groups Ministry Publishing; One LifeWay Plaza; Nashville, TN 37234.

ISBN 978-1-5359-5235-4 • Item 005814003

Dewey decimal classification: 248.84
Subject headings: CHRISTIAN LIFE / GOD / SELF-PERCEPTION

Scripture quotations are taken from the Christian Standard Bible®, Copyright © 2017 by Holman Bible Publishers. Used by permission. Christian Standard Bible® and CSB® are federally registered trademarks of Holman Bible Publishers.

To order additional copies of this resource, write to LifeWay Resources Customer Service; One LifeWay Plaza; Nashville, TN 37234; fax 615-251-5933; call toll free 800-458-2772; order online at LifeWay.com; or email orderentry@lifeway.com.

Printed in the United States of America

Groups Ministry Publishing • LifeWay Resources
One LifeWay Plaza • Nashville, TN 37234

CONTENTS

ABOUT THE AUTHORS

Stephen Kendrick (writer, producer, *OVERCOMER*) is a speaker, a film producer, and an author with a ministry passion for prayer and discipleship. He's a cowriter and the producer of the movies *OVERCOMER, WAR ROOM,* and *FIREPROOF* and a cowriter of the *New York Times* best sellers *The Resolution for Men* and *The Love Dare.* An ordained minister, Stephen attended seminary, received a communications degree from Kennesaw State University, and serves on the board of the Fatherhood CoMission. Stephen and his family live in Albany, Georgia, where they're members of Sherwood Church. Most important, as affirmed by this Bible study, he's a child of God whose citizenship is in heaven.

Alex Kendrick (director, actor, writer, *OVERCOMER*) is an award-winning author gifted at telling stories of hope and redemption. He's best known as an actor, a cowriter, and the director of the films *FIREPROOF, COURAGEOUS, FACING THE GIANTS, WAR ROOM,* and *OVERCOMER* and a coauthor of the *New York Times* best-selling books *The Love Dare, The Resolution for Men, Fireproof* (novel), and *Courageous* (novel). In 2002 Alex helped found Sherwood Pictures and partnered with his brother, Stephen, to launch Kendrick Brothers Productions. He's a graduate of Kennesaw State University and attended seminary before being ordained to ministry. Alex and his family live in Albany, Georgia, where they're members of Sherwood Church.

Nic Allen (Bible-study developer) serves as the campus pastor of Rolling Hills Community Church in Nashville, Tennessee. His undergraduate work was in communications from Appalachian State University, and he holds a master's degree in Christian education from Dallas Baptist University. His passion is to disciple kids and students while equipping parents to build stronger families.

ABOUT THE MOVIE
OVERCOMER

MEET JOHN.

When circumstances beyond his control unravel the name he has built for himself, John Harrison "becomes the least likely coach helping the least likely runner attempt the impossible in the biggest race of the year."[1]

MEET HANNAH.

She's on a journey of discovery. Like most adolescents, she wants to know where she came from, what she's good at, what it means to be part of a family, and where real value is found in life. Those are questions about identity.

Life changes overnight for coach John Harrison when his high-school basketball team's state-championship dreams are crushed under the weight of unexpected news. When the largest manufacturing plant in town suddenly shuts down and hundreds of families begin moving away, John must come to grips with the challenges facing his family and his team. Urged by the school's principal to fill in and coach a sport he doesn't know or like, John is frustrated and questions his worth until he crosses paths with a student struggling with her own journey.

Filled with a powerful mix of faith, a twist of humor, and a ton of heart, the Kendrick brothers return to theaters with *OVERCOMER,* their newest feature following *FACING THE GIANTS, FIREPROOF, COURAGEOUS,* and the number one box-office hit WAR ROOM. The inspiring family film stars Alex Kendrick, Priscilla Shirer, Shari Rigby, Cameron Arnett, and introduces Aryn Wright-Thompson. Opening nationwide on August 23, *OVERCOMER* dares to leave you filled with hope, inspired to dream, and asks the question, What do you allow to define you?

OVERCOMERMOVIE.COM

1. Jeannie Law, "New Kendrick Bros. Movie 'OVERCOMER' Based on Finding One's Identity in God, Stars Priscilla Shirer," *The Christian Post,* August 3, 2018, https://www.christianpost.com/news/kendrick-brothers-movie-overcomer-based-on-finding-identity-in-god-stars-priscilla-shirer-226556/.

FROM THE CREATORS OF WAR ROOM
WHAT DO YOU ALLOW TO DEFINE YOU?
ALEX KENDRICK
PRISCILLA SHIRER
AND INTRODUCING ARYN WRIGHT-THOMPSON
OVERCOMER
SONY/AFFIRM FILMS AND FAITHSTEP FILMS PRESENT IN ASSOCIATION WITH PROVIDENT FILMS A KENDRICK BROTHERS PRODUCTION "OVERCOMER" ALEX KENDRICK PRISCILLA SHIRER SHARI RIGBY CAMERON ARNETT AND INTRODUCING ARYN WRIGHT-THOMPSON KIMBERLY HELMS STEWART ANNA REDMON PAUL MILLS KATHERINE TUCKER ALEX KENDRICK STEPHEN HULLFISH BILL EBEL BOB M. SCOTT LARRY FRENZEL SHANNON KENDRICK AARON BURNS JUSTIN TOLLEY STEPHEN KENDRICK ALEX KENDRICK & STEPHEN KENDRICK ALEX KENDRICK
PG SOME THEMATIC ELEMENTS
OVERCOMERMOVIE.COM | @OVERCOMERMOVIE
IN THEATERS AUGUST 23
SONY
AFFIRMFILMS
FOR GROUP SALES AND ADVANCED BUYOUTS GO TO SONYPICTURESGROUPSALES.COM

INTRODUCTION

"Who are you really?" It's a fundamental question we all have to answer. Our first instinct may be to respond with a name. After that we tend to share a résumé of what we do or whom we're related to. Should we define ourselves by the members of our family or even by what other people say about us? Maybe who we are is something deeper.

Identity is what people believe to be most true about themselves. It's their source of value and worth. Tim Keller has written, "Our need for worth is so powerful that whatever we base our identity and value on we essentially 'deify.' We will look to it with all the passion and intensity of worship and devotion, even if we think ourselves as highly irreligious."[1]

If people deify or idolize whatever they base their identity on, what happens when that source of meaning fails us or is taken away? It doesn't just alter a worldview. It crushes the soul.

Enter *OVERCOMER*. Regardless of the intention with which you approach this study, the goal is a definitive answer to the basic question "Who are you?"

This Bible study, featuring group discussions, film clips, and personal studies, is designed to help you firmly establish your value and worth in Christ. You'll encounter a variety of Old and New Testament giants who either demonstrated an identity firmly rooted in God's truth or warn you of the danger of choosing alternative identities. Along the way you'll have opportunities to determine whether your identity may be ill-defined and to be drawn back to the only source of meaning in life, ever closer to Christ.

1. Timothy Keller, *The Reason for God: Belief in an Age of Skepticism* (New York: Penguin, 2018), 164.

HOW TO USE THIS STUDY

OVERCOMER Bible Study provides five lessons that can be used for group or personal Bible study. Each lesson contains four elements: "Start," "Watch," "Engage," and three days of personal study. Allow forty-five to sixty minutes for the group sessions.

START. Each study begins with an introduction to the lesson to come. This section is designed for use in a group setting but can also be adapted for personal study. Read this section and answer the introductory questions together if you're in a group.

WATCH. The Bible-study DVD contains clips from the film *OVERCOMER* to accompany each session. Each clip is two to four minutes in length and is supported by a summary of the clip and discussion questions based on the truths illustrated.

ENGAGE. This section is the primary focus of each week. Leaders should spend the majority of the group session teaching while using the verses and questions provided in this section.

PERSONAL STUDY. After attending the group session, members should complete the three days of personal study at home before the next group session. Through this personal study, group members will explore biblical content and application that support the concepts introduced in the movie clips and group discussion.

A LETTER TO LEADERS

Thank you for agreeing to lead a small group. As this study was being prepared, you were being prayed for.

What does it mean to be created in the image of God? It means the Creator, not the creation, gives us identity and purpose, determining who and what we are in the world. What does it mean to bear God's likeness in the world? It means we proclaim the praise of the One who made us, called us, and desires to use us. It means we live out a powerful declaration of who Jesus is and what it means to experience the life and salvation He alone gives.

The world around us offers insane perversions of identity. People are choosing who they want to be by living out their own misguided notions of truth. This Bible study doesn't attack those individuals. Instead, it offers a foundation that a meaningful identity can be built on, consisting of core biblical truths. We're created by God, but we're sinners. We're offered salvation that starts with repentance and leads to a life that seeks and declares Jesus as the only way to truly know and live out who we are.

Perhaps you're offering this study as part of a larger churchwide campaign anticipating the release of the *OVERCOMER* film. Perhaps your group has already seen the movie and is engaging in this study as a follow-up. Regardless of the timing of your study or the format of your group, this resource has enormous potential to lead people in your church and your community to understand and live out their core identities in Christ.

You may be experiencing anxiety or fear about leading this study. You've likely wrestled with your own identity and what it means to bear the image of God in your life. God hasn't called you to lead this study because you're a perfect disciple of Jesus. You're leading this study because God equips His people to do His work. Our prayer for you is that as you facilitate this study, you'll see God working in your life in mighty ways, and you'll sense the Holy Spirit's power sustaining you and leading you. The best way to be prepared each week is to simply complete the study yourself. Plan to be open and transparent with your group and honest about the areas in which you struggle. Pray that God will direct your conversation and strengthen you to lead well. If Jesus is your Lord, you too are an overcomer (see 1 John 5:5). Thank you for leading!

WHO ARE YOU?

*The angel of the Lord appeared to him and said:
"The Lord is with you, valiant warrior."*
JUDGES 6:12

START

Welcome to *OVERCOMER Bible Study*. If this is a newly formed group, this opening activity will help you build community and get to know one another. Even a fairly familiar group will benefit from engaging in this icebreaker.

Begin by jotting down ten things that describe who you are. They could be titles you bear, marks of personal interest, or character traits. (For example, I'm a husband. I'm a technician. I'm a student. I'm an artist. I'm a dreamer.) Use the space below to complete your list.

Go around the group and allow members to name a single item on their lists. Follow that pattern again, allowing members to read the second item on their lists. Repeat the process until each person has read aloud each of his or her items.

The identifiers from the lists composed and shared are likely positive attributes or roles. Some may even reflect God's calling, making our simple descriptions of who and what we are acts of obedience. In those cases, bravo! There's a balance between following God's will and choosing our own adventure. Yet most of what we identify about ourselves tends to be self-defined and self-designated.

MOVIE CLIP

View the first film clip. This clip not only introduces key characters but also presents the fundamental question that fuels the entire narrative. Following the clip, discuss the theme, using the steps provided.

SUMMARY

Basketball coach John Harrison enters Principal Olivia Brooks's office and learns that the football program has been terminated. The main factory in town has closed its doors, eliminating more than five thousand jobs. This closure is shrinking the town and crushing high-school enrollment. Without enough players, athletic programs are being cut. Olivia sees an opportunity to salvage the cross-country team by having John take over. In his mind cross country isn't even a real sport. But John is given the responsibility, and it begins to unravel his identity.

DISCUSS

1. What bad news does John receive in this segment?

2. Do you feel that John's reaction is to be expected and normal or too severe, considering the situation?

3. What's John forced to give up, and what's he asked to assume responsibility for?

ENGAGE

Read aloud Exodus 2:10-22. Brainstorm all of the titles and character traits that could apply to Moses.

Read aloud Exodus 3:1-6,9-14. What do these verses reveal about Moses' identity?

What changed about Moses' nature between chapters 2 and 3?

Moses lived a life of luxury as a prince in Egypt, having been rescued and raised by the daughter of Pharaoh. Consider his boldness to both the Egyptian caught in abusing a Hebrew kinsman and the Hebrew whose behavior he addressed. That's hardly the reluctant leader we encounter in chapter 3, in which we learn that Moses had become a shepherd and an everyday husband, father, and son-in-law. Moses was living a simple life under the radar until God revealed His plan to use Moses to deliver the Israelites from slavery. Moses offered a series of reasons he couldn't serve God and lead Israel. Why? The presuppositions Moses believed about himself and the opinions others would undoubtedly perceive about him outweighed who the Creator made Moses to be. He was living out an identity of his own making.

Read aloud Judges 6:6-16. What are the similarities and differences you see between Gideon and Moses?

Israel's tribe of Manasseh, named for Joseph's elder son, came in sixth of the twelve tribes in the number of fighting-age men (see Num. 26)—hardly the smallest tribe. When combined with Joseph's younger son, Ephraim, they surpassed any of Jacob's sons. However, when Israel was oppressed by Midian, Gideon claimed to be among the weakest clan in his tribe and the weakest man in his family. Yet God described Gideon as a mighty warrior.

Has God, through His Word or His Spirit, ever called you to be more than you thought possible? How did you respond?

Has the identity you built or claimed for yourself ever hindered your willingness to become who God intended you to be? How?

Who you are starts with where you came from, includes where you've been, and indicates where you're going. If your identity is scripted by Almighty God and is consistent with His Word, you're living in the truth of who He made you to be. Discovering and living that identity, as defined by God, affects everything about life. This endeavor is always worth the effort.

WHO YOU ARE STARTS WITH WHERE YOU COME FROM

Create a list of people and priorities in your life that are important to you. Be as specific as you like, but in some cases a category will suffice. For example, you can record "My family" instead of listing each individual member.

Take inventory to make sure your list is complete, including items of even nominal importance.

Now the exercise becomes more challenging. Start marking entries off your list in order, from least to greatest importance. Which ones can you live without? Narrow your list to only two or three of your top priorities. Those indicate not only what's of great worth to you but also what's absolutely vital in making you who you are.

The old expression "You are what you eat" reminds you to make wise choices about healthful eating, but it holds little weight in creating an identity. A truer phrase is "You are what's important to you."

You define yourself by your values. The problem with that truth is the word *your,* which implies your own sovereignty despite your vast limitations as a mortal. Who are you to determine who you are? Even if you have that authority, where was it derived from? Scripture has the answer.

Read Genesis 1:26.

> *God said, "Let us make man in our image, according to our likeness.*
> *They will rule the fish of the sea, the birds of the sky, the livestock,*
> *the whole earth, and the creatures that crawl on the earth."*
> **GENESIS 1:26**

What description of humanity's inherent nature and position did God offer in this verse?

God didn't wait to confer with the man to determine what his nature should or shouldn't include and what his calling or direction in life should be. God also created you to bear His image. Right from the beginning, before any of us were formed, God had a plan. For the couple in the garden, that included a definitive purpose.

Read Ephesians 2:10 and rewrite it in your own words.

These words by Paul follow a powerful description of salvation (see vv. 8-9). God has miraculously and graciously saved us to accomplish the purpose He intended.

How does knowing and being reminded of where you come from and why you were created shape your identity?

Revisit your lists for the week, both the one you created in the group session and the one you recorded at the beginning of this personal study. Which descriptions of you and values you hold are consistent with the image of God in you and the good work God planned for you?

Which ones might you need to reevaluate? End today's study by asking God to show you the priorities and pursuits you need to eliminate and the ones you need to embrace in order to define yourself by His purpose for you.

WHO YOU ARE INCLUDES WHERE YOU'VE BEEN

An important exercise for any Christ follower is to compose a gospel testimony. A basic formula is to answer the following three questions. Take time to answer these if you haven't done so lately.

What was your life like before Christ?

How did you encounter and begin to trust Christ?

What's life like now as a follower of Christ?

A well-formed Christian identity comes from an understanding of the distinct truth that God Almighty created us to bear His image and to follow His purpose. It also includes a keen, ready recognition of where we've been. All of us began by living a life of sin and rebellion. Only when we trust Christ does He begin to redefine our identity.

Along the way Israel suffered many consequences for its frequent refusal to live according to God's plans. That disobedience was sin. Why did people who had tasted God's goodness drift and adopt an identity apart from God's design?

Examine Genesis 3:1-6. In this early snapshot of human history, the first man and woman chose to believe a lie. Why did they do that? Based on what you read, specifically in verse 6, why did the couple succumb to the serpent's temptation?

Are there patterns of sin in your life that formed because you've believed lies? Explain.

Are there patterns of sin in your life that formed because you chose your own pleasure and what you perceived to be good? Explain.

Read Daniel 1:1-7.

It wasn't enough to take over a nation in Nebuchadnezzar's day. To ensure long-lasting dominance, the culture of the ransacked nation had to be replaced by that of Babylon. It was an effective leadership strategy. Nebuchadnezzar selected leaders from the displaced people group and set out to influence them first.

What were the criteria for Nebuchadnezzar's chosen influencers among the Israelites?

The elements of the royal table in Babylon would have been prohibited by Jewish dietary laws. Later in the chapter Daniel and a few friends requested permission to avoid the rich diet. The implicit fact is that many of Israel's elite gave in. Was it the lust of the eyes, the lies of the enemy, or the overwhelming pressure from their new surroundings that caused the unnamed young men to give in?

All of us have been in a place where something or someone has lured us away from God's plan. Although that's an awful place to remain, it's not a bad place to recall. Knowing where you've been points you to forgiveness and gives God an opportunity to display the attributes of His character that you need most.

If your sinful state has been repented of and forgiven, recalling the darkness of that place provides good motivation never to return. An identity characterized by forgiveness makes the best foundation for your life today.

Pray about any patterns of sin you identified today. Confess and ask God to forgive you and to show you changes you can make to align your life with His plan. If you've already received God's forgiveness for ways you've departed from His purpose, thank Him in prayer today.

WHO YOU ARE ULTIMATELY INDICATES WHERE YOU'RE HEADED

In the group session you described who you are with declarative titles. Perhaps you identified yourself by your family role, such as a parent, or by a professional role, such as a teacher. Maybe you opted for more personal characterizations or hobbies, like a dreamer or a reader.

How does the way you describe yourself shape the direction of your life?

When a person operates in an identity other than the one God intended, how does that identity affect the direction his or her life takes?

Recall your study of Moses and Gideon from the group session. Both Old Testament heroes were blessed by a relationship with God. He defined who they were and determined where they went.

Read Exodus 3:12-14. What promise did God make to Moses?

What did knowing God's name provide for Moses?

Read Judges 6:16-22. What similar promise did God make to Gideon?

How did God illustrate who He was to Gideon?

In what ways has God promised you His presence and revealed
His identity to you?

Review your list of priorities in day 1. How do God's presence
and identity script your priorities?

When identity is rooted in God's truth, Christ followers don't just know who
they're meant to be. They more clearly see who God is and the path He lays
out for them to take. In Psalm 32 David's summary of his life and connection
to God's plan could easily describe both Moses and Gideon. It's a good
description of our lives too.

Close this week by carefully reading Psalm 32. What qualities did David
mention that you'd like to be true of your identity?

Moses and Gideon were more than forgiven. They were called. They abandoned misunderstanding and followed God's instruction. In God they were
deemed righteous.

Psalm 32:7 wonderfully applies to both Moses and Gideon. For God to be a
protective hiding place, He must be near. God called Moses and Gideon not
only to be people they didn't think they could be but also to go to places
they didn't think they could go and to accomplish tasks they felt ill-equipped
to accomplish. In addition, He promised to be with them along the way.

Who does God want you to be? What does He want you to do?
How confident are you to move ahead, knowing He's with you?
If you're unclear about the answers to these questions, simply ask
God to speak. Ask Him to give you ears to hear, a heart to obey,
and a willingness to take risks in order to go where He leads.

YOU ARE BROKEN

My people have committed a double evil:
They have abandoned me,
the fountain of living water,
and dug cisterns for themselves—
cracked cisterns that cannot hold water.
JEREMIAH 2:13

START

Welcome to group session 2 of *OVERCOMER Bible Study*. Begin by asking for responses to last week's personal study.

What stood out to you in last week's personal study? What truths or answers did God reveal?

Describe a time when a difficult circumstance turned out to be good for you. Consider the following questions as you formulate your response.

How did you initially react to the event?

How did God prove Himself faithful in this circumstance?

How did you grow and learn from the experience?

Unexpected change and difficult circumstances are routine occurrences in life. When calamity comes, your responses can expose the real you. The way you react to adversity often reveals something about your nature, exposing layers of brokenness that previously lurked unnoticed. This circumstance then becomes a great opportunity to grow. This week's study will highlight that truth. Pray together as you prepare to watch the film clip.

AFFIRM Films A Sony Company © 2019 C*

SUMMARY

Circumstances have a way of circumventing our best-laid plans. That's the case for John and Amy. As the ripple effect of the factory's closing continues to upset the Harrisons, the place where John has built his identity is revealed. Amy, his wife, knows it and has a less-than-gracious way of approaching the subject. John certainly needs accountability, but high stress is taking a toll on the marriage. During a moment of marital reproof, difficult words are exchanged, and brokenness in John's heart is exposed.

DISCUSS

1. Whose is the more difficult situation—John's or Amy's? The person going through the life-altering circumstance or the person watching the one he or she loves navigate those changes? Explain your response.

2. How do you think John felt when he heard those words from Amy?

3. Do you find it easier to be the person offering reproof, regardless of the tact, or the person receiving it?

ENGAGE

Invite someone to briefly share the events of Jonah 1–2. Then read aloud Jonah 3–4, using several readers if necessary.

According to chapter 3, what happened when Jonah delivered God's message to the Ninevites? According to chapter 4, how did Jonah feel about this result? What "I told you so" message did Jonah declare?

From Jonah's perspective, the story doesn't end well. When God spared the people of Ninevah, the prophet viewed it as the worst possible outcome. He had just publicly declared that God would destroy them, and now his reputation was on the line. He also knew the Assyrians were an exceedingly wicked, violent people who deserved God's wrath. But Jonah was also aware that in the unlikely event the Ninevites repented, God might show grace and relent from judgment. And Jonah was greatly disappointed to see that the fireworks show of God's wrath had been canceled. When the book closes, a people who had been very far from God had come very near, and a man who should have celebrated this return was so disgusted that he wanted to die.

What's your gut reaction when God does or allows what you don't like or expect? What does your response reveal about your character and identity?

The Ninevites' brokenness was overtly displayed in expressions of sin and rebellion. Jonah's brokenness was hidden inside a calloused part of his heart. To you, is one more dangerous than the other? If so, which one? Why?

Read aloud Jeremiah 2:1-13. Discuss similarities between this period in Jeremiah's ministry and the Jonah narrative. Do you notice any differences?

Today we might call the Ninevites of Jonah's ministry an unreached people group. They were faraway, foreign enemies of God who needed a missionary to come, identify sin, and explain the path to salvation. The sinful Judeans described in Jeremiah 2 were a people of God who should have known better. In a time of comfort, they built an identity outside the promise of being God's children, and sin crept in. Elevating anything above God's place is idolatry. God's people were guilty, and Jeremiah's job was to let them know.

Why is it good when our brokenness or idolatrous identity is revealed?

Who you are starts with where you came from, includes where you've been, and indicates where you're going. It's also best displayed when you face trials or, as in Jonah's case, don't get your way. Although exposing and exploring brokenness is difficult, Scripture points out that it's ultimately good for us.

WE'RE BROKEN BECAUSE THE WHOLE WORLD IS

Ninevites are everywhere. Scrolling through Twitter or watching world news indicates that wickedness abounds. Pause to consider the state of the world today. Don't linger too long, though. It's difficult and depressing.

It's easy to spot examples of sin in false religions, pagan countries, and developing nations. The proverbial "they" is a readily available target. Here at home it's easy to put blinders on and hide behind the assumption that we live in a Christian nation. Our country, however, is equally and collectively just as broken and in need of repentance as foreign ones. We have individually and collectively moved far from God.

Read Jeremiah 2:1-13.

Examine each verse and identify specific ways God's message to Jerusalem applies to your life. For example, have you ever felt like the description in verses 2-3? Describe it.

Review verses 5-9. Have you been or are you currently walking in a season like the one depicted, when you stopped seeking God and turned in another direction? Describe it.

Rewrite verse 13 in your own words.

Record the broken wells in which you've placed your trust and found your identity. As you do, utter a prayer of confession about each one.

Read the following verse.

> *Woe is me for I am ruined*
> *because I am a man of unclean lips*
> *and live among a people of unclean lips,*
> *and because my eyes have seen the King,*
> *the LORD of Armies.*
> ISAIAH 6:5

Our individual brokenness is a microcosm of what's wrong with the entire world. Trading the goodness of God's plan for our own individual desires is sin. Furthermore, it never leads to the abundance God desires for us.

Underline the portion of Isaiah's confession in which he recognized his individual sin. Circle the portion in which he announced the broader sin of his whole people group. Which sin came first?

Although it's often easier to recognize brokenness everywhere else, it's better to start with ourselves. These facts of individual and universal sin aren't mutually exclusive. They operate in close conjunction. People are broken because the world is broken. The world is broken because each individual has embraced sin by choice and by nature. That broken nature becomes evident when we place our hope, our faith, or our identity in any well other than God's. Acknowledging that truth about ourselves is a step toward healing.

Thank God for using the brokenness in your life to reveal your need for Jesus. Ask Him to heal the brokenness in the world and in your life.

WE'RE BROKEN BECAUSE WE CHOOSE TO BE

You know that person in your life whose faith through difficulty both inspires you and scares you? You stand in awe of them, wondering how they could remain so strong when their particular trials seem far too heavy. You also shudder in fear, confessing you can't imagine being that strong. Perhaps you've even thought, *I don't think I could walk through that experience and still trust God.*

Whoever that person is, their trial is so grueling that most people would be inclined to give them an automatic pass from faith-filled living due to the severity of their circumstance. Maybe you perceive John and Amy Harrison's predicament through that lens. His anger and frustration are certainly understandable. Brought to that point, many of us would respond similarly. However, understandable doesn't equate with permissible or beneficial for followers of Jesus.

Calamity reveals where we place our hope and the foundation on which we've built our identity. The way we respond to trouble indicates who we are and whom we trust. People are broken not only because the world is broken but also because we choose broken systems and broken paths in our lives.

Read Jonah 4. Summarize what God offered Jonah as well as Jonah's response to God.

God's offer:

Jonah's response:

God extended grace to Jonah, only to be rejected. God appointed the prophet Jeremiah to bring His word of warning to wayward Judah. The nation's collective response was similar to Jonah's individual one.

Read Jeremiah 18:1-12.

Have you ever consciously or subconsciously chosen to remain broken, wallowing in pity and declaring your right to do so? Describe that season in your life.

Read Deuteronomy 30:15-20.

Isolated, this passage could easily be construed as a foundation for works-based salvation. However, salvation is still God's great gift of grace, and in no way can it be earned. This passage isn't about good behavior. It's about faithfully believing that God's way is the best way and that eternal life isn't just in heaven but here on earth as well. This passage reveals the power of choice that lives within the realm of faith. We can't always choose our circumstances or even the outcomes of those circumstances, but we can always choose the way we respond. Either we can either embrace God's grace, or we can reject it and choose sin.

Does a particular area of your life reveal that you haven't chosen the wholeness of God's plan? It's easy to recognize choices that aren't Christlike. Describe the broken cistern you've chosen for yourself.

How could you choose to embrace grace in order to give a godly response in this difficult situation?

Reflect on the areas of your life in which you've chosen your way over God's way. Regardless of the consequences you've faced, thank God for being with you and remaining faithful. Ask Him to help you live the life He created you to live.

DAY 3

WE'RE BROKEN, BUT WE CAN BE HEALED

Coming face-to-face with our brokenness can manufacture a wide array of outcomes. We can reject the idea of our brokenness and declare our identity as a personal right or an individual choice. Or we can admit that we have no way to fix ourselves and that we need God's grace and mercy, freely available in Jesus Christ, to save us from ourselves. We may even waver back and forth between two commitments, trusting in God's design one day and in our own ambition the next.

Ultimately, our goal is freedom from our brokenness. Because people are broken, we often choose to remain that way and build identities on false foundations. Our lives don't have to be that way. God has another plan. The storm could have swept Jonah away. The fish could have done more than just swallow the prophet. It could have digested him. God provided Jonah a way out and illustrated His great mercy in the way He addressed Ninevah and in the way He continued to lovingly lead Jonah.

God offers rescue from our brokenness today. He can heal our broken hearts and desires. He promised to do that for His stubborn children in Jeremiah 18. And Scripture offers more examples.

Read the following verses.

> *The men of the city said to Elisha, "My lord can see that even though the city's location is good, the water is bad and the land unfruitful." He replied, "Bring me a new bowl and put salt in it." After they had brought him one, Elisha went out to the spring, threw salt in it, and said, "This is what the Lord says: 'I have healed this water. No longer will death or unfruitfulness result from it.' " Therefore, the water still remains healthy today according to the word that Elisha spoke.*
> 2 KINGS 2:19-22

Elisha, the prophet who followed Elijah, was barely inaugurated into the role when the people of Jericho approached him with a problem. The location of their camp was good, but the water was bad. They needed a miracle. God made the water clean and safe to drink again, meaning the barren land could bear fruit again.

Identify the areas of your life in which you most need healing.

The way we respond to pressure excavates levels of brokenness in our lives that may have been hidden previously, buried far beneath the surface. We can fake it, making it from one seemingly normal day to the next, but when crisis comes, the truth unravels, and the foundation of our lives shakes.

Where did your brokenness come from? How have circumstances brought it to the surface?

The ultimate remedy for brokenness is forgiveness, but we can't receive forgiveness until we recognize our need for it. Brokenness is often the tool God uses in our lives to help us realize our great need for Him. In this process of recognizing our true identity, we also truly understand repentance. There's a big difference between being sorry for wrongdoing and experiencing true sorrow over our sin. The former is a recognition of an unfavorable result, while the latter admits the underlying root of our sinful condition. Once we've recognized the root of our sinful heart, we're ready to accept forgivenss and be made new in Christ.

Record a prayer expressing your need for God's healing in your life. Confess ways you've been stubborn and unrepentant. Ask for complete freedom from sin through God's forgiveness.

YOU
ARE
CHOSEN

He chose us in him, before the foundation of the world,
to be holy and blameless in love before him.
EPHESIANS 1:4

START

Welcome to group session 3 of *OVERCOMER Bible Study*. Begin by asking for responses to last week's personal study.

What stood out to you in last week's personal study? What truths or answers did God reveal?

Describe a time when someone chose you. Maybe it was a fourth-grade pickup game, when you were the new kid in town and terrified of being picked last. Maybe it was a special prom invitation. Perhaps it was something life-altering like a scholarship or a marriage proposal. How did it feel to be wanted and chosen?

The degree of excitement increases with the seriousness of the purpose for which a person is chosen. Neighborhood kickball may be a big deal at the moment, but it hardly compares to being chosen to deliver the keynote address at your college commencement. The significance of being chosen also increases with the importance of the person making the selection. When that person is the holy Creator God of the universe, the significance of being chosen is unfathomable.

MOVIE CLIP
View the film clip for this session.

AFFIRM Films A Sony Company © 20

SUMMARY

The backstory of principal Olivia Brooks and young Hannah runs deeper than this brief clip can convey. Seizing a moment to check in on Hannah and everything spinning in her life gives Olivia an open door to present the gospel. As Hannah wrestles with feelings of abandonment toward her earthly father, Olivia explains the great lengths that her Heavenly Father went to in redeeming her. Miraculously, Hannah receives Jesus.

DISCUSS

1. What part of Olivia's gospel presentation stands out most to you?

2. How confident do you feel about conversationally presenting Christ to someone? Give yourself a score from 1 to 10, with 1 being completely paralyzed and 10 being completely prepared.

ENGAGE

Read aloud 2 Chronicles 3:1-4,8-9,14-17.

Solomon followed through with God's call and his father David's instructions to construct the temple in Jerusalem. It would replace the tabernacle where the ark of God's covenant promise was housed and where the people engaged in sacrificial worship. The temple would give God's place in the community a sense of permanence and priority. Many people might skim or avoid the passages that provide detailed descriptions of that work, but many of those details point to Jesus. For example, the exterior columns were given names. The name Jachin means "He will establish." The name Boaz means "Strength is within Him." The pillars served as a physical reminder that it was God who established Israel in strength. It's God who chooses, saves, and strengthens. He does that through salvation.

Christ's birth brought God's full presence to reside with us. That's why Jesus is called Immanuel, "God is with us" (Matt. 1:23). Christ's death tore the curtain of the holy of holies in the temple, giving us full access to God, inviting us to be established as God's people, clothed in His strength (see 27:51).

What does it mean to you that the God who created you wants to be right here with you? How does God's choosing you and desiring to be with you give you strength? How does God's choosing you change the way you see yourself and others?

Read aloud John 3:16-17. What word or phrase resonates most with you?

Read aloud Ephesians 2:1-10.

Ephesians 2:1-3 describes identities rooted in sin instead of the Lord. Verses 4-10 describe what it means to chosen by God.

According to this passage, how does God save people?

Read aloud again verses 5-10 one at a time and identify specific reasons God saves people.

The gospel is the good news that God chooses to love and save people. How overwhelming to know that the great God of all has chosen broken people to receive His love and purpose! Being chosen and defined by God changes everything.

The Gospel Changes Your identity and Gives You a Purpose

In the film *OVERCOMER* the gospel of Jesus gave John Harrison a purpose beyond who or what he thought he was. When the foundation on which he had built his identity was ripped away and replaced by something less than ideal, the gospel entered and gave him more than he ever knew he wanted. The gospel pulled Hannah out of the shadows and gave her a purpose far beyond what her physical limitations prescribed. The gospel of Jesus has the power to change a person's identity and to give purpose in life beyond all limitations and expectations.

Solomon was one of Israel's most famous kings, second only to his father, David.

Read 1 Chronicles 22:7-10.

What does this passage say about Solomon's true identity?

What does this passage identify as God's purpose for Solomon?

How clearly do you understand God's purpose for your life? Use the spectrum provided to pinpoint your current level of awareness and plot an *X* on that spot.

| No idea what my purpose is | Fully aware of and living out my purpose |

Your identity in Christ makes you God's child, enjoying all of the rights and blessings of sonship. Your purpose in life makes you God's servant, dedicating your life to following His will.

According to God's words to David, Solomon wasn't just the king of Israel's son. Solomon was a child of God with a clearly defined purpose. This isn't true just for homegrown kids like Solomon who were born into the right religious family. It's true for the very enemies of God, like Saul in the Book of Acts, who was dramatically changed by an encounter with Jesus to become a Christ follower. That's good news for us.

Read Paul's testimony in Acts 22:3-16. Where did Paul place his identity before meeting Christ?

For some people, a life-changing experience on their own Damascus road will be exactly how God reaches them. For others, life before Christ wasn't as dramatically distant and didn't require that level of encounter. No matter what type of testimony you have, change is part of it. Paul himself wrote:

> *If anyone is in Christ, he is a new creation; the old has passed away, and see, the new has come!*
> 2 CORINTHIANS 5:17

Record some before-and-after changes the gospel has made and is continuing to make in your identity and your purpose.

Post and reread 2 Corinthians 5:17 several times throughout the week. Use it as a reminder of the power of the gospel to change your life. Pray that God will keep your newness in Christ fresh this week. Pray that God will plant this verse in your life and that He will shape your identity to reflect its truth.

DAY 2

THE GOSPEL CHANGES YOUR COMMUNITY

An online search for the definition of *community* offers these ideas:

• A group of people living in the same place or having a particular characteristic in common (for example, the scientific community)

• A feeling of fellowship with others as a result of sharing common attitudes, interests, and goals (for example, the sense of community that organized religion can provide)

Those two definitions sum up community pretty well. People likely have a variety of different pockets of community, some that overlap and others that don't seem to intersect.

List your personal pockets of community. Be as inclusive as possible. Give a name or label to every type of community you feel a part of.

For believers, it's ultimately the gospel that connects us, gives us a family, and defines what it means to be a family. The gospel gave Hannah a coach who was far more than a coach and a principal who was far more than a principal. It ultimately reconnected her with an earthly father whom she could love and be loved by. It gave her a community and a place to belong.

When Christ died, He didn't just give us salvation, though that was more than enough. He also gave us the Holy Spirit and much more. He gave us the church. The gospel changes who we are and whom we're connected with. The gospel gives us a community of faith that supports us in Christ, encourages our growth in Christlikeness, and holds us accountable to Christ's call in our lives. People who are united by the gospel need one another.

Read 1 Peter 2:9-10 and record everything the writer declares believers to be.

Notice that every declaration is plural. Peter didn't declare a Christian to be a royal person or a holy individual. Each layer of his promise-filled declaration is applied to the body of Christ, the church.

Read Hebrews 10:19-25.

The first part of this passage discusses our nearness to God through Christ. Then the writer highlighted the necessity of our nearness to one another because of Christ.

In your own words, how does the gospel give you community and encourage you to be part of a community?

In what ways does community help you live out the gospel?

Praise God for expressions of the gospel in community. Thank Him for people who've represented the gospel well to clearly show you Jesus, both recently and throughout your life.

THE GOSPEL CHANGES YOUR OUTLOOK

Recall the most extravagant gift you've ever given someone. What was it, and to whom did you give it?

In all likelihood the gift you described was temporary. Unless you thought of a time when you shared the plan of salvation, anything you exchange in life has an expiration date. Nothing surpasses what Christ accomplished on the cross. On the cross He took on all our sin and brokenness and gave us a new identity that's secured by His sacrifice on our behalf. Nothing is better than that.

God gave His absolute best when He offered Christ as the payment for our sin. Paul gave his absolute all in communicating that message of hope to the whole world. The gospel isn't just for eternity, though. It's for everyday living. The gospel doesn't just alter a person's forever. The true gospel shapes a person's outlook every day.

Peter is a prime example of a transformed outlook. His encounter with Jesus caused him to recognize his own tragic sin.

Read Luke 5:1-11. How did Peter respond to Jesus' net-casting instructions?

How did Peter react to the crazy boat-breaking catch? Why do you think that miracle prompted Peter to respond the way he did?

Peter did what Jesus asked in that moment. He followed Jesus. So much water went under the bridge in Peter's ministry with Jesus following that initial call. So much living. So many stories. So many great miracles and challenging teachings. Peter would later fail miserably, but the gospel restored him and empowered him to faithfully carry out his calling in the early church.

Read Acts 10:9-16,34-35.

An angel visited a faithful Gentile named Cornelius and instructed him to reach out to Peter, whose vision prepared him for the encounter. Following Peter's vision described in verses 9-16, servants arrived and took Peter to Cornelius, who told Peter about the angel's visit. Peter's response was to present the gospel. Prior to that encounter, like the other Jewish Christians, Peter believed the gospel was strictly intended for Israel. Not only was Peter's life changed by the gospel, but his everyday outlook was also influenced by following Jesus.

In the movie *OVERCOMER* what felt like the worst thing to happen in the town, particularly to the school and the Harrison family, was the best thing to advance God's purposes in the gospel. Sometimes when we face difficulty, the outcome reveals that a better, more gospel-centered purpose was at play.

Read the following verses.

> *Blessed be the God and Father of our Lord Jesus Christ. Because of his great mercy he has given us new birth into a living hope through the resurrection of Jesus Christ from the dead and into an inheritance that is imperishable, undefiled, and unfading, kept in heaven for you. You are being guarded by God's power through faith for a salvation that is ready to be revealed in the last time. You rejoice in this, even though now for a short time, if necessary, you suffer grief in various trials so that the proven character of your faith— more valuable than gold which, though perishable, is refined by fire—may result in praise, glory, and honor at the revelation of Jesus Christ.*
> 1 PETER 1:3-7

In a letter to dispersed and discouraged believers, Peter offered words of encouragement. Their disaster was an opportunity for the gospel to spread to places and to people Peter would have previously counted unworthy. That change in Peter's outlook and in early church history is one only the gospel could have fostered.

Describe something about your life that has changed or is changing because of the gospel.

Pray, identifying the parts of your outlook that need to be touched by the gospel. Ask God to change your perspective so that you see the world and even yourself as He does.

YOU SURRENDER

You rejoice in this, even though now for a short time, if necessary, you suffer grief in various trials so that the proven character of your faith—more valuable than gold.
1 Peter 1:6-7

START

Welcome to group session 4 of *OVERCOMER Bible Study*. Begin by asking for responses to last week's personal study.

What stood out to you in last week's personal study? What truths or answers did God reveal?

Share with the group the person who asks you the toughest questions. This may be your spouse, your accountability partner, or your mentor. Who forces you to evaluate who you are, where you're going, and what your journey means?

Discuss the way those relationships initially formed, whether they're formal (planned, set meetings for mentoring and discussion) or informal (living life together and engaging with important topics as they emerged), and the perceived benefit of having that person in your life.

WATCH

WATCH

View the film clip for this session.

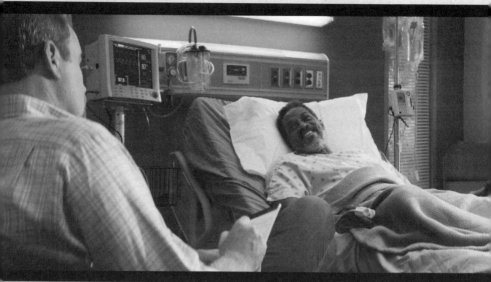

AFFIRM Films A Sony Company © 2019 CT

SUMMARY

Playing the hand life dealt doesn't mean John automatically embraces the change. At this point in the film, John still laments the loss of his basketball team and the possibility he saw on that path, including a state championship win and a scholarship for Ethan. When Thomas, his unlikely new friend, asks that key question "Who are you?" John leads with basketball even though it's gone.

DISCUSS

1. Why do you think Thomas, at this point in his life, can enter this depth of conversation with someone like John, who was so recently a total stranger?

2. Is it easier or more difficult to hear and consider questions like Thomas's from someone you're close to or from someone new in your life? Explain your response.

3. Why do you think the question was so difficult for John to answer? How closely can you relate?

ENGAGE

Read aloud Matthew 16:13-20.

Peter was specifically called and created to build the church of Jesus—not a purpose you would imagine from a career fisherman. He quickly adapted to the role of disciple, being the first to proclaim Christ as Savior and also among the first to fail at living out that confession. His conversation with Jesus in Matthew 16 shows that it isn't what others claim about Christ that matters. It's what each of us believes that matters.

According to Jesus, who revealed Peter's revelation to him, and why does that fact matter?

If you had eight floors of elevator conversation with a stranger who asked you, "Why do you believe in Jesus?" how would you respond?

Your belief in or confession of Christ is more than just words. In your day-to-day relationships and interactions beyond a five-minute gospel pitch, a surrendered life speaks louder and communicates better. In Peter's life we see actions that authenticate his confession of faith and others that contradict it. He's an everyman type of disciple we can all relate to.

Read aloud Luke 22:31-34. Why do you think Jesus declared the good Peter would do to build the church after the miserable failure that was coming?

Have you ever feared you would be disqualified from fulfilling God's purpose in your life because of your mistakes? How do you wrestle with that?

Peter's later denial of Jesus came each time he was identified as one of Christ's followers (see Luke 22:54-62). Christians should be easily and readily recognized as followers of Jesus. Our allegiance to Him should be the most obvious truth about us. For others to easily identify us as disciples of Jesus, we must walk closely with Him and root our identity in Him. Living out our identity in Christ is the only way to be fully alive. Otherwise, we're guilty of practical atheism, claiming Jesus with our mouths but living life as if He doesn't exist.

In what ways is it obvious that you follow Jesus? In what ways do you hide your commitment to Him?

When we identify ourselves first and foremost as followers of Jesus, we'll live a life of faith that makes our connection to Jesus one of the most prominent features of our lives. Other people will notice.

DAY 1

PETER READILY FOLLOWED JESUS

"Because I said so" might be a phrase from your childhood home that you vowed never to repeat to your children. Before you take such a hard turn, let's evaluate it from a different perspective. According to the wisdom of God Almighty and His infallible Word, parents are the divinely appointed authority in a child's life. "Because I said so" can communicate that we know best and lovingly care for our children through limits and instructions.

Read Luke 5:1-11.

Peter's "Because You said so" obedience in verse 5 is a model for us. His repentance in verse 8 is a challenging inspiration to us. His sacrificial decision to follow Jesus in verse 11 is an unparalled sign of authentic surrender.

Read the following verses and rewrite them in your own words as confessional declarations to God.

> *"Master," Simon replied, "we've worked hard all night long and caught nothing. But if you say so, I'll let down the nets."*
> LUKE 5:5

> *When Simon Peter saw this, he fell at Jesus' knees and said, "Go away from me, because I'm a sinful man, Lord!"*
> LUKE 5:8

> *They brought the boats to land, left everything, and followed him.*
> LUKE 5:11

Each verse conveys an aspect of surrender. The first is ready-made obedience when the instruction seemed pointless. Peter was a professional. He knew fishing. Yet because Jesus said to lower the nets, he obeyed.

Describe a time when God asked something of you that seemed wild, when you thought you knew better, or when His instruction didn't seem to make practical sense?

It's important to note that Peter didn't question or hesitate. Remember Moses and Gideon's reluctance? Peter's ready-made obedience is refreshing and inspirational. That obedience also led to radical repentance—in other words, worship—in verse 8. Finally, the act of obediently following Jesus and going fishing in a moment and a manner that didn't make sense birthed a willingness to leave what was familiar in order to follow. Is each of these responses evident in your life?

Where do you or would you like to see radical obedience in your life?

Where do you or would you like to see radical, repentant worship in your life?

Where do you or would you like to see radical, willing sacrifice in your life?

Read again Luke 5:5,8,11. As you do, invite the Holy Spirit of God to craft each form of surrender in your life. Then pray, expressing your desire to readily follow Jesus. That means taking on His character, His truth, and ultimately a new identity.

DAY 2

PETER BOLDLY PROCLAIMED JESUS

Ultimately, life isn't about us or our own agendas. John the Baptist best summed up the essence of surrender:

> *[Jesus] must increase, but I must decrease.*
> JOHN 3:30

Jesus must always increase. We must always decrease. Peter had it right when he declared that Jesus was "the Messiah, the Son of the living God" (Matt. 16:16). In response to Peter's confession of faith, Jesus said:

> *You are Peter, and on this rock I will build my church,*
> *and the gates of Hades will not overpower it.*
> MATTHEW 16:18

What if Jesus intent wasn't to build the church on the man Peter but on his confession of faith? Jesus once explained that the disciples would do even greater works than He did (see John 14:12). That's a hard pill to swallow, but by confessing our trust in Christ, we surrender to His grand plans for our lives and for His kingdom. Peter experienced the fulfillment of Jesus' promise firsthand in a ministry that spanned three decades and included its own share of miracles. In this way Christ's plan to build His church was carried out by a fully chosen, fully surrendered people.

What's your confession of Christ calling you to be and build in His name? It may be something small that He can multiply for His glory or something huge that's far beyond your reach.

Have you ever felt compelled to boldly declare your connection to Christ or communicate the truth about Jesus, but you shied away from the opportunity? If so, describe that experience.

Have you ever felt compelled to boldly declare your faith, and you shared the gospel truth with someone? If so, describe your experience.

Copy Jesus' words to Peter in Matthew 16:18.

Read Acts 4:1-12. In this defense Peter referred to Jesus as the cornerstone (see v. 11). Considering Jesus' promise to build the church on the rock of Peter's confession, why is it significant that Peter used the word *cornerstone?*

In a sense Peter was reminding the Sanhedrin of the authority of the words in Psalm 118:22 by connecting Jesus to the great King David and the holy Hebrew Scriptures. He was clearly, unequivocally declaring that Jesus is the One in whom light, life, and salvation are found. And he was making that bold declaration from the dark shadow of a possible prison sentence.

What's the greatest risk you've faced or the greatest loss you've experienced because of Jesus? Was it worth it? Would you do it again? What would you do differently?

To boldly declare Jesus in the face of fear is to believe that the world needs more of Him and less of you. It's to believe that any risk you take in confessing Christ will be worth it.

Pray, boldly proclaiming that you want more of Jesus in the world and less of you. Dedicate your life to representing Jesus rather than yourself.

DAY 3

YET PETER STILL DENIED JESUS

Matthew 16 was a win for Peter. He must have clung tightly to that moment. Without hesitation Peter proclaimed Christ as Savior. Jesus' prophecy for the future church must have been affirming. And yet denial remained on the horizon for Peter.

Read the full account of what happened in Luke 22:31-34,54-62.

Epic fail. If Matthew 16 is the episode you never want to forget, Luke 22 is one you hope no one remembers. It's easy to get caught up in the pendulum of vacillating faith. While being boldly surrendered in one moment, we know the enemy is ready to attack our weak spots, causing us to deny the most essential truth in our lives. Peter denied Jesus in a moment of weakness and fear but later boldly proclaimed Christ to an audience who had their own reasons to be afraid.

What are your self-prescribed legitimate fears? What might cause you to occasionally define yourself by "I can't" or "I'm not"?

In his first letter to dispersed Christians, Peter articulated his understanding of fear. Knowing the temptation to deny Jesus would be fierce, he wrote these words:

> *You are being guarded by God's power through faith for a salvation that is ready to be revealed in the last time. You rejoice in this, even though now for a short time, if necessary, you suffer grief in various trials so that the proven character of your faith—more valuable than gold which, though perishable, is refined by fire—may result in praise, glory, and honor at the revelation of Jesus Christ.*
> **1 PETER 1:5-7**

Paraphrase that passage in your own words. Then read it aloud. Hear the promise of hope offered by someone who knew what it was like to be on top, as well as what it was like to be crushed by anxiety in the moment.

Which is better for you—a friend who tells you without hesitation that everything is going to be OK or someone who comforts you but understands and verbally recognizes your difficult circumstances?

In this brief passage Peter did both. Underline the part in which Peter boldly declared, "God's got this." Circle the part in which Peter recognized that the believers would face hardship.

Consider the final part of this passage, the concept of being refined by fire. Temperatures upwards of one thousand degrees Celsius literally burn the impurities from raw, extracted gold until only purity remains. Peter won in Matthew 16. The pressure was on and the fire was hot in Luke 22. It burned, but it molded Peter more closely into the image of Jesus, fashioning him into the leader he needed to be in order to lead God's church. Is it possible that we need Luke 22 moments as much as we need Matthew 16 ones?

Pray, thanking God for difficulties in life. Tell Him that being shaped more closely into the image of Jesus is worth the hardship.

YOU DECLARE

Everything that was a gain to me, I have considered to be a loss because of Christ.
PHILIPPIANS 3:7

START

Welcome to group session 5 of *OVERCOMER Bible Study*. Begin by asking for responses to last week's personal study.

What stood out to you in last week's personal study? What truths or answers did God reveal?

List as many emotions as you experience in a given week. Then take turns reading your lists. When identical ideas are presented, place check marks beside the ones on your list. When it's your turn again to share, read only new items that haven't been previously named.

Emotions are incredible gifts from God. He bestows them for His pleasure and to give us ways to know and express ourselves and relate to others. Unchecked, however, emotions can become barriers to our true identity. Sometimes our senses and feelings deceive us, leading us to believe lies and establish an identity that deviates from God's promise for our lives.

It's one thing to know your identity is in Christ. It's another to be prepared for the attacks that will come. We learned from Peter that being firmly rooted today doesn't guarantee success tomorrow.

How important is boldly declaring who you are in Christ directly to the enemy when he erects an unforeseen barrier in your way or brings a personal attack against you? Are you prepared to contradict your feelings and act from your true identity?

AFFIRM Films A Sony Company © 2019

SUMMARY

The Hannah we see in this week's clip is decidedly different from the young girl we encountered two weeks ago. Armed with faith in Christ, Hannah confidently begs for the question, ready with her answer. Hannah is certain of her worth because her identity is no longer rooted in the father who deserted her, the asthma that plagued her, the sin that followed her, or the sport that defined her. She now boldly declares her relationship with Christ and her citizenship in heaven. Her identity is wrapped up in Jesus.

DISCUSS

1. How is Hannah different? What changed?

2. What spiritual truth revealed by Hannah in this segment do you resonate with most? What part of her declaration did you need to hear most?

3. What are you still wrestling with in regard to your identity? What still competes for God's prominent place in your life?

Engage

In Exodus 32 Moses was missing. The wilderness-wandering Israelites knew he was meeting with God on Mount Sinai, but they were concerned about how long he had been gone and whether he was coming back. So they reverted to what they would have seen and done in Egypt: they fashioned an idol and worshiped it. God was ready to pour out His final judgment, but Moses interceded and then displayed a little righteous wrath of his own.

Read aloud Exodus 32:11-20. How did Moses plead with God? Why did it matter that Moses rooted his argument in God's promises?

How did Moses discipline Israel?

How was Moses different in this passage from the Moses who made excuses in Exodus 3:11-14? What do you think changed?

Only when we fully understand, embrace, and operate from our identity in Christ can we accomplish the tasks God has planned for us. That requires life change along the way. Because Moses cited God's promise in His people's defense, he was declaring that he knew and accepted God's call on his life as a leader and God's purpose for His rescued people. Moses understood that this plan was part of the promise God had made ages before.

In Judges 7 Gideon was now leading an army. The Lord instructed Gideon to whittle down the army from thirty-two thousand soldiers to only three hundred. Why? So that the victory would be unmistakingly God's. On the eve of the battle, God instructed Gideon to spy on the Midianite camp.

Read aloud Judges 7:13-18. How did this Gideon differ from the one we first encountered in Judges 6:6-16? Why do you think he changed?

Why was the conversation Gideon heard important to him? How did he respond and invite people to respond after he heard it?

Gideon still valued confirmation, and God was gracious to oblige. At the conclusion of these verses, Gideon boldly declared in faith that God would bring victory. He went from defending his own fear and weakness to leading an army in confidence. Why? He believed God. How? He abandoned his old, useless identity and embraced the man God said he was.

You too are invited to work out your own identity in Christ. Then you can celebrate your bold declaration for the Lord and for His servant—you!

Paul Had an Old Identity

Paul vividly described the transition from the old identity to the new identity this way:

> If anyone is in Christ, he is a new creation; the old has passed away, and see, the new has come!
> **2 CORINTHIANS 5:17**

When Paul wrote, "The old has passed away," he probably intended to convey the meaning of the old adage "Gone but not forgotten." We don't forget who we used to be apart from our identity in Christ. But we actively choose not to live in that identity any longer.

In this final week of personal study, we'll explore the transformation that occurred in the life of Paul.

Read Philippians 3:3-14. Name the reasons Paul considered himself the ideal Jewish leader in verses 4-6.

You can almost hear Coach Harrison exclaim in the principal's office, "I'm not a cross-country coach! I'm a basketball coach!"

What we identify as the sin of idolatry and a false identity was rooted in the persona of a devout man doing what he thought was right in the eyes of Israel's God. Paul gave a litany of qualifications that defined his identity, exposing his confidence in fleshly things, even pitting himself against anyone else as someone who had more reasons to be proud.

You've already exposed the sinful foundations of your life through this Bible study. Many of them were probably just attempts to be the best person you could possibly be.

What are some good, even God-honoring pursuits people find their identities in? What labels are used in the church to elevate people over simply being crucified with Christ?

The misplaced priorities in Paul's life were hurdles only an encounter with Jesus could overturn. Similarly, any false identities in your life have prevented you from establishing a firm foundation in Jesus and from aligning your goals with God's purposes.

Describe Paul's new goals in life, outlined in verses 7-14.

Record any new goals you've set for your life, based on your experiences over the past five weeks in this study.

Record a prayer asking the Holy Spirit of God to help you overcome obstacles to fully realizing your identity in Christ and to make your Christ-honoring goals a reality.

DAY 2

PAUL FOUND AND ROOTED HIS LIFE IN FAITH

Moses wrote five books to express all of the mighty deeds God did to establish His people. His song in Deuteronomy 32 expressed that gratitude, along with his farewell words. Try to imagine these words put to music:

> *I will proclaim the LORD's name.*
> *Declare the greatness of our God!*
> *The Rock—his work is perfect;*
> *all his ways are just.*
> *A faithful God, without bias,*
> *he is righteous and true.*
> **DEUTERONOMY 32:3-4**

Remember in Exodus 3:13 when Moses asked God for His name? Here in this song Moses proclaimed it loudly! Deuteronomy 32:3-4 sounds as if it belongs in any modern praise chorus. The rest of the song? Not so much. From verse 5 nearly all the way to the end, Moses highlighted Israel's sin as much as God's power. This final declaration was hardly from a man who lived in fear. He passionately issued a warning to his people about the consequences of living contrary to their true identity in the Lord God.

If your study over the past few weeks could culminate in a warning for yourself and others, what would it be?

By the time the events in Acts 28 occurred, Paul had already been shipwrecked, diverted, arrested, tortured, imprisoned, and worse. Yet the chapter closes with the apostle welcoming people and boldly declaring his faith in Jesus. It sounds as though he had quite a few reasons to recant, but none of his circumstances could erase his identity in Christ.

Read Acts 28:30-31.

Basically under house arrest, Paul spent two years in a rented house displaying a beautiful picture of Jewish hospitality to everyone who visited, for the express purpose of declaring God's goodness in providing salvation through His Son, Jesus. Once you find that treasure, you can have joy even in the worst moment.

Verse 31 says Paul witnessed "with all boldness and without hindrance." Copy that phrase here.

What do you think it means to live a life that declares faith "with all boldness"?

What does it mean to have no hindrance?

"Without hindrance" translates the Greek word *akolutos,* which means "to prevent, to hinder, to forbid, to withhold, to deny."

Denial.

"I'm not a good speaker."—Moses

"I'm not a strong fighter."—Gideon

"I'm not a cross-country coach."—John Harris

"I'm not _____."—You

We can share Jesus "with all boldness and without hindrance" when we stop denying who we are in Christ. In Jesus we can overcome any obstacles that get in our way of living fully rooted in faith and passionately sharing that faith without hesitation. Do you believe that? Does your conviction show?

Confess your "I'm not ..." statements to Jesus and leave them with Him. Praise God for making you an overcomer, not by your might but by the transformational power of the gospel.

PAUL WAS MADE NEW AND LED FROM A POSITION OF STRENGTH

Peter wrote about faith that's refined by fire (see 1 Pet. 1:7). The process is similar to exercise. Muscles that are unused eventually atrophy. Exercise builds muscle and strength by actually tearing down muscle fibers. When the body recovers and the muscles rebuild, they're stronger. Breaking down muscles makes them stronger.

When you consider the danger, turmoil, and difficulty Paul faced, it's not hard to see why his spiritual muscles grew strong. Though developed in difficulty, Paul's faith was rooted in his confession of faith in Jesus Christ, birthed from his life-changing encounter with the risen Lord.

Who's more inspiring to you—believers fervently following Jesus with no scars or marks of their trials or believers with deep wounds who remain radically faithful? Explain your answer.

Read Paul's words that follow.

[The Lord] said to me, "My grace is sufficient for you, for my power is perfected in weakness." Therefore, I will most gladly boast all the more about my weaknesses, so that Christ's power may reside in me. So I take pleasure in weaknesses, insults, hardships, persecutions, and in difficulties, for the sake of Christ. For when I am weak, then I am strong.
2 CORINTHIANS 12:8-10

Highlight each word that conveys hardship.

Even while Paul was in prison, people recognized Christ in him and were changed. His faith under fire was inspiring, and he leveraged it to share Christ without fear or hindrance. Others were inspired to proclaim that same gospel, and Paul rejoiced even in his own affliction because Christ was being declared. That result makes adversity worth the cost.

Though our worldly identity can easily lead to pride, our identity in Christ exposes the sheer strength of living faithfully in spite of outside adversity and inner weaknesses. Because celebrating adversity and heralding our weakness are the opposite of the world's tendency, they're shocking.

When you think of Coach Harrison, fast-forward and imagine the possibilities. Imagine his testimony five years later, coaching a new state-champion runner, profusely thanking God for taking away basketball and his misplaced identity. Observing the way his faith developed in that season of fire could have a great impact on someone else who faced a trial.

Summarize any life change you've experienced during this Bible study.

What outcomes do you hope for as you leverage what God is doing to refine you and to solidify your identity in Christ?

Thank God for any life change you've experienced through this study. Pray that in the future, the way you see yourself and the way other people see you will be colored by Jesus.

ADULT RESOURCES & FAMILY BIBLE STUDIES

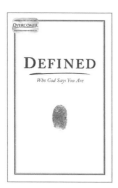

Defined: Who God Says You Are
By Stephen Kendrick and Alex Kendrick
from B&H

Based on the main theme of the movie *OVERCOMER*, this book from best-selling authors Stephen and Alex Kendrick helps adults understand the importance of finding their true identity in Christ.
Paperback | $16.99 | 978-1-5359-4892-0
Definido: Quién dice Dios que eres
available in Spanish, September 2019
Paperback | $12.99 | 978-1-5359-66832

Defined Bible Studies
from LifeWay Resources

Just as Hannah turns to Ephesians in the movie *OVERCOMER* to understand who God created her to be, this series of studies will help everyone in your church or your home dig deeper into the themes found in this powerful book.

Defined Leader Kit for Adults
Includes DVD teaching from the Kendrick Brothers, plus a workbook
Retail Product, Boxed - $99.99 - 978-1-5359-7013-6
Defined Bible Study Book, the companion to the *Leader Kit*
Paperback | $13.99 | 978-1-5359-7013-6

Overcomer: The Novel
from Tyndale

Award-winning fiction author Chris Fabry teams up again with Alex and Stephen Kendrick to deliver a heartwarming novel based on the *OVERCOMER* movie. The novel will enrich your expérience with the film, telling you more about the characters you'll meet in the movie. See the movie! Read the book!
Hardcover | $25.99 | 978-1-4964-3861-4
Paperback | $15.99 | 978-1-4964-3862-1

Teen Resources

Radiant: His Light, Your Life
(for Teen Girls) - from B&H
by Priscilla Shirer

Beloved author and speaker Priscilla Shirer plays Principal Olivia
Brooks in the movie *OVERCOMER*. Her latest book is written to
help teen girls understand they can find their identity in Christ.
Paperback | $12.99 | 978-1-5359-4987-3

Revealed: Discovering Your True Identity in Christ
(for Teen Guys) - from B&H

Alex and Stephen Kendrick, along with writer Troy Schmidt,
lead teen guys on a hands-on investigation to uncover who
they really are and how Christ has shaped their identities.
Paperback | $12.99 | 978-1-5359-4988-0

Defined Bible Study for Teen Girls
Ephesians Bible study by Priscilla Shirer (includes kit and workbook)
Paperback | $13.99 | 978-1-5359-6006-9

Defined Bible Study for Teen Guys
Ephesians Bible study by Stephen and Alex Kendrick (includes kit and workbook)
Paperback | $13.99 | 978-1-5359-6007-6

Children's Resources

Wonderful: The Truth about Who I Am
(for Middle-Grade Readers) - from B&H Kids
Stephen Kendrick and Alex Kendrick, with Amy Parker, have written this
illustrated book for middle-grade readers to help them discover who they
are and how God has made them to be unique and wonderful.
Printed Hardcover | $12.99 | 978-1-5359-4988-0

What's So Wonderful about Webster?
(Children's picture book) - from B&H Kids
By Stephen Kendrick and Alex Kendrick
A fully illustrated picture book, this story about Webster's field-day adventures
helps young readers discover that they too are wonderfully made by God.
Hardcover Picture Book | $12.99 | 978-1-5359-4986-6
Release date: November 19, 2019

Defined Bible Study for Kids
Paperback | $14.99 LG | $6.99 KABs - 978-1-5359-5679-6
Also featured: Leader's Guide, Younger Kids Activity Book, and Older Kids Activity Book

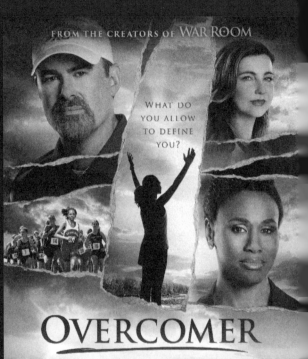

OTHER BIBLE STUDIES FROM MOVIES BY ALEX AND STEPHEN KENDRICK

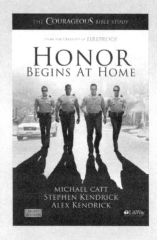

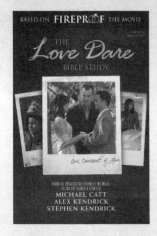

WAR ROOM BIBLE STUDY

Learn about the power of prayer and expand your group's understanding of spiritual warfare with this five-session Bible study based on the film with the same name.

HONOR BEGINS AT HOME

Build on the message of the *COURAGEOUS* movie and create a new legacy of faith with this 8-session small group Bible study.

THE LOVE DARE BIBLE STUDY

Discover God's amazing design for marriage and enrich the relationships of the married couples in your group with this Bible study based on the film *FIREPROOF*.

LifeWay.

LIFEWAY.COM | 800.458.2772